Recovering
in the Tao

Tao

The Way to Healing and Harmony

Recovering
in the Tao

The Way to Healing and Harmony

Eric D. Greene

Tao Bear Books
Wayne, Michigan

Published by
Tao Bear Books
Wayne, Michigan 48184

Cover design and illustrations by Jacob Stevens Corvidae

Printed in the United States of America

LCCN 2002091029
ISBN 0-9719361-0-2

Dedication

To Gia-fu Feng: *Although you are gone, your voice continues to guide me. Your simple message plays over in my mind and is echoed in the wind, the moon, and the stars. And it is there you live on, forever at one with the Tao.*

To Suzanne "Susie" Braun: *You taught me more about recovery than anyone, but now you are gone, too. I will always treasure the time we had together and the love we shared.*

Acknowledgements

I am greatly indebted to the following people, who each played a significant role in the creation of this book:

All of the Twelve-Steppers whose honesty, experience, hope, and strength helped to move my recovery forward.

Roxana Marsh, for reviewing the manuscript and for your useful suggestions.

William Martin, for your wonderful endorsement and valuable advice.

Jacob Stevens Corvidae, for your great artwork and enthusiasm.

Tree Bressen, for your excellent proofreading and valuable critique.

Norma Schonwetter, for your helpful consultations.

My parents, Ray and Myra Greene, for helping me to get situated after my recent long journey. I look forward to continued growth in our relationship.

My best friend, David Tacey, for your support, validation, and friendship. I have been very blessed to have you in my life.

Contents

Introduction   ix

One   The Origin of Disharmony   1

Two   Trying to Fill the Void: 19
             The Spectrum of Addictions

Three   Harmonizing Our Relationships   45

Four   Learning to Go with the Flow   69

Five   Living the Tao   99

References and Resources   117

Introduction

Taoism is an ancient Chinese philosophy that advocates simplicity and harmony. The legendary founder of this philosophy is Lao Tzu, who is believed to have lived in the sixth century B.C. The essence of Taoism can be found in Lao Tzu's classic book, the *Tao Te Ching*, or "Book of The Way and Virtue." I have come to regard the *Tao Te Ching* as a wonderful recovery book, for its primary purpose is to help guide the people of the world back to a state of harmony, serenity, and wholeness.

The concept of "Tao" (pronounced *dow*) is very difficult to explain. In fact, Lao Tzu begins the *Tao Te Ching* by saying, "The Tao that can be told is not the eternal Tao." The word, "Tao," has been translated as "The Way," or "The Path." I like to think of Tao as "Ultimate Truth," or "Ultimate Reality." Put simply, Tao is what works. Tao is what *is*. Tao is not "God," as in the Western notion of God the Father, the creator and divine ruler of the universe. Tao did not create the universe. It *is* the universe. It is also the way the universe operates.

"Recovery" is a healing process, which many people call, "the journey to wholeness." During this process, we come to terms with what happened to us when we were growing up, how those experiences helped shape our lives, and how our behavior may have affected those around us. We also learn to take risks, let go of old roles, release our "toxic shame," and start to love and accept ourselves unconditionally.

I use the words "dysfunction" and "disharmony" almost interchangeably, because the more dysfunctional our upbringing, the more we tend to resist the flow of the Tao, which throws us into a state of disharmony. As we begin to heal our childhood wounds, we become once again like conduits—capable of allowing the creative forces of the universe to flow through us without resistance.

I refer to the central figure in this book simply as the "Taoist." The "Taoist" is a highly developed individual who exists in harmony with the world. Although this person is largely modeled after my teacher, Gia-fu Feng, we all have the potential to become the "Taoist." Hence, I avoid the use of a strictly male archetype.

Writing this book has helped me to continue moving forward in my recovery, and I hope reading it does the same for you. Like any recovering person, I still struggle at times, but it has been my experience that such growing pains are unavoidable. As I continue to grow and heal, I find myself moving ever closer to harmony with the great Tao.

— Eric D. Greene

| One |

The Origin
of
Disharmony

The Origin of Disharmony

All of us come into this world whole, complete, and in perfect accord with the Tao. In order to maintain this harmonious state, we would need parents who are able to perfectly meet every one of our developmental dependency needs. We would also need to be raised in a society that can continue to perfectly meet all of our needs, as we begin to break away from the nest.

Since people and societies are not perfect, these conditions can never be satisfied. The result is that a spiritual wound is created. This spiritual wound, passed down from generation to generation, is the origin of disharmony.

Bad Karma

T ransgenerational migration of behavior is a fancy term that means to transfer our dysfunctional behavior, and thus our spiritual woundedness, to our children. This process is similar to a parent passing on a virus or a genetic predisposition to a child. The important thing to remember is that the child is an innocent victim. We are all innocent victims. The spiritual wound we carry around is not of our making.

Another way to view this phenomenon is that parents pass on their *bad karma*[1] to their children, who then have to spend their entire lives working it off. The karma that is not worked off is then passed on to the next generation. Of course, we can still work off our bad karma even after we have infected our children with it. To work off our bad karma, we must begin a long healing process—a process that will ultimately lead us back to harmony with the Tao.

---

[1] *Karma*, in Sanskrit, means *action;* thus *bad karma* translates to disharmonious action, or dysfunctional behavior.

Toxic Shame

The bad karma we pass on to our children has another name: *toxic shame*. Toxic shame is passed down from parent to child through abandonment, abuse, and neglect. The abandonment may be physical or emotional. The abuse may be physical, sexual, or emotional. The more sensitive a child is, the more toxic shame he or she will internalize.

The size of our spiritual wound, or "soul-hole," is directly proportional to the amount of toxic shame we internalized as a child. As we recover, we will begin to release our toxic shame, and our spiritual wound will gradually become smaller.

Shamelessness and Conscience

When we are toxically shamed, we become *shameless*. John Bradshaw divides shamelessness into two categories: "righteous shamelessness," where a child grows up to be arrogant, pompous, judgmental, and totally self-absorbed, and "depraved shamelessness," where a child becomes overly dependent, unmotivated, slothful, and self-abusive. In both cases, the child does not develop a healthy sense of shame.

A healthy sense of shame means to be in touch with our conscience. Our conscience manifests as guiding feelings. These feelings include embarrassment, guilt, remorse, and humility. Toxic shame is so powerful that when we are experiencing it, most other feelings become swamped out, especially the subtle feelings of healthy shame.

Healthy shame, or conscience, is what keeps us connected to the real world—to Tao. When this connection is lost, we are forced to take our guidance from the abstract world of laws, principles, and morals, and from our own emptiness and pain.

The Principles of Opposites and Relativity

The principle of yin and yang, the two opposing forces that underlie the entire universe, is central to Taoist philosophy. *Yang,* the male element, is associated with movement, brightness, and creativity. *Yin,* the female element, is associated with stillness, darkness, and dissolution.

The two opposing forces that underlie our psychospiritual lives are "divine love" and "toxic shame." These two basic elements are similar to feelings in that we know and understand them by experiencing them. When one experiences divine love, one feels secure, nurtured, whole, and serene. When one experiences toxic shame, one feels empty, abandoned, defective, and anxious.

The principle of yin and yang is inextricably linked to another Taoist concept—the principle of relativity. Relativity means that all pairs of opposites arise together and define each other. Thus, we can never have yin without yang; nor can we ever have yang without yin. For example, we only know what "long" is in relation to "short." The same is true for "inside" and "outside," "bright" and "dark," "life" and "death." It is therefore necessary to have some toxic shame in the world if we are to know and experience divine love.

"More Than," "Less Than"

All toxically shamed people have low self-esteem. As a result, they go through life feeling that they are "less than" other people. Many of them try to compensate for this feeling by striving to be "more than" other people.

"More-thans" tend to overfunction in their relationships and are extremely independent. "Less-thans" tend to underfunction in their relationships and usually find a "more-than" to become dependent upon. Occasionally, "more-thans" and "less-thans" will switch roles. And it is also quite common to be a "more-than" in some of our relationships and a "less-than" in others.

As we begin to love and accept ourselves unconditionally, our self-esteem will rise, and we will no longer find ourselves playing the role of "more-than" or "less-than." We will become *interdependent* in our relationships: We will be able to depend on others when we need them, and they will be able to depend on us when that is appropriate. By harmonizing yin and yang in this way, our lives will become more balanced, and our relationships will become much healthier.

Shame and Blame

There is an interesting relationship between shame and blame. Many people with low self-esteem, both "more-thans" and "less-thans," tend to place a lot of their self-worth in external things. They also tend to be perfectionists. When things go wrong and mistakes are made, they can become so consumed with toxic shame, they either deny a mistake was made, or they try to shift the blame to someone else. They also tend to be unforgiving when others make mistakes, and they often try to pass on their toxic shame to them.

The Taoist does not place her self-worth in external things. If she makes a mistake, she readily admits it. She may feel ashamed or embarrassed, but she does not experience the sting of toxic shame, and she does not attempt to shift the blame to anyone else. She also allows others to make mistakes, which gives them the freedom to try new things and to grow. In this way, she is passing on her divine love.

We Love the World the Way the World Loved Us

There is a passage in the Bible that states, "We love him, because he first loved us."[1] In other words, we love God with God's own love. In childhood, for all intents and purposes, our parents are God. They are the alpha and the omega of our entire existence. We are completely dependent upon them for all of our physical and emotional needs.

Children who are brought up in very loving environments are full of self-love, and they are able to give this love back to their parents. They are also able to pass this love on to their siblings, friends, schoolmates, and later, to their *own* children. Conversely, children who are raised in very shaming environments are full of self-hatred, and they have very little love to give back to the world.

If we are only able to love the world and ourselves the way the world loved us as a child, are we to be stuck with this anemic love for the rest of our lives? Maybe. This is where recovery comes in. As we travel along the recovery road, we will begin to convert toxic shame into divine love, and in doing so, we can love the world *better* than the world loved us.

---

[1] 1 John 4:19

9

Unmet Needs Breed Neediness

When basic childhood needs go unmet, the groundwork is laid for a lifetime of *neediness*. For example, children who are not accepted by their parents may spend their entire lives looking for acceptance—usually from those who cannot or will not accept them either. Children who are not held and lovingly touched tend to look unceasingly for this physical affection, and when they finally do receive it, they often become addicted to the person who is giving it to them.

Among the most basic childhood needs are *narcissistic needs*. Children must be loved and accepted unconditionally, and they must be told how wonderful, special, and unique they are. When narcissistic needs go unmet, children will often become very egocentric—obsessed with creating an image of themselves they can feel good about.

When children's natural needs go unmet, they may spend their entire lives trying to meet these needs in unnatural ways. This can result in a lifetime of disharmony and pain.

Using Is Abusing

Children from dysfunctional homes are often robbed of their innocence and exuberance at a very early age. One way parents strip children of their divine nature is by using them to fulfill an adult need they are unable to get fulfilled by another adult. All such using of children should be considered abuse.

When parents use their children as their best friends, they remove the generation gap that is necessary for children to develop properly. Children should not be told the intimate details of their parents' love life or of their financial problems. And they should never be put in the middle of an argument between two adults.

Using children to take on adult responsibilities is another way children are deprived of their childhood. This includes children who work too hard trying to earn money, who parent other children, and who take care of too many of the household chores. And, of course, any kind of incest, whether it is overt (physical) or covert (emotional), is the most egregious example of using and abusing a child.

We should never use a child to meet an adult need or responsibility. Conversely, adults must meet the needs of their children. Children are divine creatures who exist in harmony with nature and should not be robbed of this state prematurely.

Children Are Like Mirrors

C hildren are like mirrors. When they are in a functional situation, they reflect the love and nurturing that has been given to them. When they are in a dysfunctional environment, they simply reflect the dysfunction around them. In psychological terms, they are *the overt manifestation of the covert family dysfunction.*

Children reflect their family dysfunction in two ways: They either act it out or they act it in—and sometimes they do both. *Acting out* means doing things to get attention or approval, or releasing anger in inappropriate and destructive ways. *Acting in* means to hurt oneself physically or to punish oneself emotionally. Both types of behaviors are an attempt by children to exert some control over their lives, since they often feel powerless when they are in their home environment.

We should treat all children with the same love and respect, regardless of whether they are acting in or acting out their family dysfunction. When they are able to process it, these children can be given new information, and they can begin to break the cycle of dysfunction.

Dysfunction Flows Downhill

M any parents like to blame their children for *their* problems. These guilt trips are not only damaging to a child's emotional and psychological development, they are in direct opposition to natural law. Just as water always flows in a downward direction, dysfunction always flows down from the older generation to the younger. When children act out, they can make life very difficult for their parents, but as I have already stated, they are simply reflecting their family dysfunction and "loving" their parents with the same "love" that was given to them.

The dysfunction that is passed down from parent to child includes unresolved issues, unexpressed anger and grief, the inability to communicate needs and other necessary relationship skills, and above all, toxic shame.

We must come to terms with our own dysfunction and that of our family of origin. Once we do this, we will be able to break the cycle of dysfunction, and we and our children can begin to live healthier, more spiritual lives.

April Fool's Joke

I magine that someone you know very well runs up to you, and with great emotion, tells you your house is on fire. As you frantically drive home, you are full of fear and anxiety. Finally, you locate the source of the smoke—a barbecue in the back yard. Suddenly, people jump out of the bushes yelling, "April Fool! April Fool!"

All of the stress, anxiety, and fear one experiences during an April Fool's joke feels real, even though it arises from a false belief. This is exactly what happens when one is raised in a dysfunctional family. All babies come into this world as wonderfully divine, angelic little creatures, who exist in perfect harmony with the Tao. Unfortunately, many parents play a horrible trick on their children. They make their children feel as if there was something wrong with them—as if they were some sort of mistake. Most of the stress, anxiety, and fear we experience in life comes from the deep down belief that we are not okay. It would be wonderful if our parents called us on the phone one day and laughingly explained that they had played an April Fool's joke on us, and that their parents had played the same joke on them.

Regardless of what we have done or what our defects are, we are okay, and we always have been. The moment we realize this, we are completely recovered; we are completely whole; we are in complete unity with the Tao.

14

Pushing Back the Finish Line

I can remember being told at the age of five that Kindergarten was important because it prepared me for First Grade. Later, I was told that First Grade was designed to prepare me for Second Grade. Second Grade was designed to prepare me for the ever-important Third Grade. Third Grade was really important because.... You get the picture. Then I was told that High School was important because it prepared me for College. College was important because it trained me for a career. And once I became established in a career, I was told to work hard and eventually good things would happen such as promotions and raises. At some point, I figured out that this game never ends, because the finish line is always being pushed back!

There is nothing wrong with working hard and learning, as long as we are not engaging in these activities to try to "become somebody" or to try to "make something out of ourselves." When we can accept and love ourselves for who we are, we will have reached the finish line, and we will have won the game!

Perfectionism

Perfectionism will be defined here as trying to change or control who we really are, and not allowing ourselves to make a mistake. Simply put, "who we are" is the sum total of our feelings and experiences. Children who are not allowed to freely express themselves tend to deny certain feelings and experiences. They often rationalize their feelings—deciding how they *should* feel, rather than simply trusting what they are truly feeling. Children who are not allowed to make a mistake are reluctant to take risks and try new things. They also tend to remain on guard at all times, to make sure they don't slip up.

Perfectionism can result in a host of physical problems such as ulcers, headaches, insomnia, and a knot in your gut; it can cause emotional problems such as chronic worrying, nervousness, anger, depression, fear, and stress; it can manifest as neuroses such as compulsive cleaning and excessive personal hygiene.

It is important that we own our feelings and experiences, and permit ourselves to make mistakes. When we can do this, we will have moved significantly forward on our journey to wholeness and harmony.

Going into Hiding

When we are not allowed to simply be who we are, our delightful inner child goes into hiding. We form a protective shell around him or her. We rarely let anyone in. We trust few. We will not allow ourselves to be vulnerable. We will not allow ourselves to be hurt anymore.

When we are not permitted to be who we are, we also tend to create false images of ourselves and false personalities to go with them. Over time, we can forget who we really are and completely lose contact with our inner child.

The Taoist is comfortable with who she is. Being comfortable with who she is, she is in touch with her divine inner child. Being in touch with her inner child, she exists in harmony with the entire universe.

Rigid Thinking

T hose who grew up in very rigid environments tend to be very rigid thinkers. They think in absolute terms, "This is this" and "That is that." There is no wiggle room—no flexibility. Such rigidity of thinking allows them to believe they are in control of things; but this is just an illusion.

The universe cannot be explained in absolute, or concrete, terms. It is both yin *and* yang, this *and* that, yes *and* no, as well as all that lies in between. The universe is also very fluid, and any attempt to cling to it is futile. Trying to control the universe by clinging to thoughts—principles, beliefs, opinions—is also futile and only serves to create a blockage.

Thoughts arise by themselves. They drift into our minds like waves lapping onto the shore. We can play with them for a while, but then we must allow them to recede back into the ocean of the great Tao.

| Two |

Trying to Fill the Void

The Spectrum of Addictions

Trying to Fill the Void

C hildren who are spiritually wounded feel empty inside. They have a large and painful hole that reaches into the very depths of their souls. Since nature abhors a vacuum, these children are driven to try to fill this void. Once this process begins, the seeds of addiction are planted.

This chapter explores the many ways we try to escape our feelings, medicate our pain, and fill the void. It also provides an overview of the entire addictive process and describes how addictive behavior throws us into a state of disharmony with the Tao.

Escaping and Isolating

There are many methods children use to escape their feelings and isolate from a dangerous world, including fantasizing about being a hero or celebrity, creating fantasy friends, forming secret clubs and secret languages, and the ultimate escape...suicide.

When things get too crazy, a lot of children will run away or find a place to hide out for a while. Some children are able to psychologically "check out." They have out-of-body experiences, where they float away to a safe and peaceful place, or else they simply stare at a wall or mirror until they "disappear."

Children who grow up in very dysfunctional environments learn to stuff their feelings or to unconsciously dissociate from them. As a result, many of these children remain emotionally numb, while others go through life angry, sad, depressed, or anxious.

We cannot be fully in the present when the ghosts from our past are still controlling our behaviors and our moods. We must therefore undergo a healing process and connect back to feelings and events that were too painful to deal with as children. Once the ghosts are eliminated, we can enjoy our remaining days and years in unity with the Tao.

Drugging

Another way we learned to cope with the pain of our childhood was to drug ourselves. I will use the term "drugging" to refer to any behavior we engage in for the purpose of medicating, or distracting us from, our feelings and our pain. There exists an entire spectrum of drugging behaviors that may later manifest as addictions. Such behaviors include the misuse of narcotics, alcohol, work, food, sex, gambling, money, power, shopping, television, relationships, exercise, and many others too numerous to mention.

It is important not to judge ourselves too harshly for engaging in this sort of behavior when we were growing up. Drugging served a useful purpose inasmuch as it allowed us to survive in a dysfunctional environment. But like escaping and isolating, the use of drugs causes us problems today. Without coping skills, we may be unable to make important decisions, handle daily stresses, and work out solutions to problems. Our addiction to our drug or drugs often becomes the most important part of our lives. We tend to neglect our health and the health of our family, as well as many of our adult responsibilities. We may even resort to lying, cheating, and stealing to secure a "fix." Furthermore, most addicts believe life would be totally unlivable without their drugs.

Dependency upon drugs represents a spiritual bankruptcy. Ridding ourselves of our dependencies is an important step in our journey to wholeness and harmony.

Control

People from dysfunctional backgrounds often seek to control and manipulate those around them. They do this for a variety of reasons: to ensure a steady supply of drugs; out of a fear of abandonment or of making a change; they have poor communication and boundary-setting skills; managing other people's lives distracts them from the pain and emptiness of their own lives; they get off by controlling and dominating others.

The universe has a natural order to it, which the Chinese call *Li* (pronounced *lee*). When we attempt to control too many things, we disrupt this natural order, we destroy the creative process, and we lose our way. By allowing people and things to follow their natural course, we follow our own natural course—to harmony with all things.

The Cycle of Using and Shame

When addicts come down from a high, they often feel ashamed about using, about neglecting their responsibilities, and about their unhappy lives. To alleviate these uncomfortable feelings, they often turn once again to their drugs; thus they become stuck in a cycle of using and shame.

Sometimes addicts will isolate when using their drugs. At other times, they will use with addicts who share their drug of choice. They may even try to get nonaddicts to use with them if possible. They do this to try to mitigate the shame of using, for they delude themselves with the belief that if other people are doing it, it must be okay.

The Taoist stays with and works through any painful feelings he experiences. He does not seek to medicate them. He therefore does not become stuck in a vicious cycle of using and shame.

Addiction: Nature or Nurture?

Generally speaking, our genes determine *what* we will become addicted to, and our childhood environment determines the extent to which our addictions will manifest. The term "drug of choice" is therefore misleading, since we do not actually choose our drugs…. They choose us.

I can remember as a young teen experimenting with different drugs—marijuana, hashish, alcohol—looking for something to make me feel okay. None of these substances worked. I was not genetically predisposed to them. What did work, I later discovered, was gambling and fantasy. I played poker almost every day and went to the racetrack every weekend. I fantasized about being a hero and about girls. This worked. This medicated my pain. This got me high. This made me feel okay…for a while.

When we first encounter our drug of choice, usually by accident, many of us will feel okay for the first time in our lives. We feel powerful. We feel complete. We become hooked! Any freedom of choice we may have had in our lives is now gone, for the addiction is in control. We will use our drugs until the pain of using exceeds the pain we are attempting to medicate. For many, the pain of their woundedness is so great, this never happens. These poor souls ultimately die in their addictions, after living hellish lives in disharmony with the Tao.

Two Basic Components to Addiction

There are two basic components that underlie all addictions: the *biochemical* and the *psychospiritual*. The biochemical component is a function of our genetic makeup and determines *what* we will become addicted to. The psychospiritual component refers to the spiritual wound we carry around that was formed in childhood. The greater our woundedness, the stronger our addictive tendencies will be.

The biochemical component produces the rush you feel when your drug of choice is in front of you. It is what causes every cell in your body to cry out, "I want that! And I want it now!" It causes the shortness of breath, the fluttering heart, the sweaty palms, and the loss of concentration. It is also what activates the pleasure centers in the brain that give us our "high." The psychospiritual component has many names: "the great void," "the hole in the soul," "the wounded inner child." This emptiness is what fuels our addictions. But the more we try to fill the void, the deeper it becomes.

It is important to mention that simply understanding the process of addiction does not make us any less of an addict. As we begin to heal, however, we are able to reduce the environmental, or psychospiritual, component, which makes it easier to quit using. We are, and will always be, powerless over the genetic, or biochemical, component.

Obsession and Compulsion

To repeat, there are two basic components to addiction—the biochemical and the psychospiritual. The way these two elements tend to manifest is through *obsession* and *compulsion*. For the purposes of this book, obsession will be defined as the unhealthy clinging to a thought, feeling, or desire. Compulsion will be defined as the acting out of an obsession.

Obsession and compulsion are inextricably linked, and together they present a formidable challenge to all recovering addicts. When addicts are not actively using, they are often thinking about using. And if they allow themselves to obsess long enough —if they allow themselves to engage in enough "stinking thinking"—they may soon find themselves using once again. When an addict or an alcoholic refers to the "monkey on his back," he is referring to obsession and compulsion.

The Taoist acknowledges all thoughts, feelings, desires, urges, and cravings, and then lets them drift through him without acting upon them. In this way, he does not give them any power.

Core Issues

C ore issues are deeply rooted problem areas that result from childhood traumas, unmet childhood needs, and toxic shame. Most of the dysfunction in our lives, including many of our obsessive and compulsive tendencies, can be traced back to our core issues.

Examples of childhood experiences that can later manifest as core issues include abandonment and loss; abuse by authority figures; lack of love and physical affection; not being permitted to express feelings such as anger and grief; not being trusted. Left unresolved, our core issues will continue to plague us our entire lives. When one of our core issues comes up, we tend to become very afraid or angry, and we often overreact to the situation. We also become very susceptible to relapsing in our addictions.

The Taoist has identified and continues to work on her core issues. When one of them crops up, she sees it as an opportunity to grow and heal.

Switching Addictions

M ost of us consider ourselves to be recovering when we have given up one particularly destructive addictive behavior. The fact is, however, unless we have identified and are working on our core issues, we are not really recovering, but have merely switched our addiction. It is like taking a pile of dirt from your living room and sweeping it into your bedroom. You can tell the world your house is clean, when in reality you have simply moved the pile of dirt around.

People in recovery programs are notorious for switching their addiction to the program itself. In fact, this may be a good thing, for it buys us some time to discover and to work on our core issues. Once we have begun to address our core issues, we may still find ourselves relapsing in one addiction or switching to another. Recovery, however, is about "progress—not perfection."

Addictive Society

We live in a very addictive society. To some degree, we are all addicts. The reason we do not know this is because we have drugs for "good" people and drugs for "bad" people. The "good" people are addicted to religion, morality, money, rules, and laws. Since they have most of the power, they have conspired against the "bad" people—substance abusers, gamblers, and sex addicts.

Even among substance abusers there are "good" addicts and "bad" addicts. The prescription drug abusers and their suppliers, doctors and pharmaceutical companies, are doing everything legally and therefore have the blessings of society. The cocaine, heroin, and marijuana users and their suppliers are acting illegally and therefore are "bad." We use sex to sell almost everything, with beautiful, scantily clad women and men adorning the covers of most magazines and popping up on nearly every television station. Yet those caught engaging in irregular sexual behaviors are subject to scorn and public ridicule.

In truth, there are no "good" addictions and there are no "bad" addictions. There are just addictions. Until we are able to grasp the big picture, we will continue to be a society of addicts— one addict persecuting another. Since a society is comprised of many individuals, as more of us start to recover, we can create a much more enlightened and spiritual society.

Addiction to Foods and Chemicals

The use of foods and chemicals to alter our moods and to escape our problems is so prevalent in this society, it is not surprising that so many of us are addicted to one or more substances. These substances include salt, sugar, cola, chocolate, caffeine, fatty junk foods, nicotine, cocaine, marijuana, heroin, prescription drugs, alcohol, paints, glues, diet pills, and anything else one might be inclined to inhale, ingest, or shoot up.

It is important to determine what our motivation is for using certain foods and chemicals, and if we have become addicted to these substances. If we determine that we do have a problem with a particular substance, it is *we* who must decide to seek out help, for an important recovery axiom states, "Recovery is not for those who need it; it's for those who want it."

Although substance abuse is a problem, it is almost always a symptom of a much greater problem—an empty and painful life. Once we begin to address our core issues and heal our childhood wounds, our lives will become richer and more fulfilling, and our need to medicate with foods and chemicals will gradually diminish.

Addiction to Fantasy

It is perfectly natural for young boys and girls to engage in fantasies. Some children take this behavior to an unhealthy extreme, however. These young fantasy addicts spend hour upon hour in isolation—medicating the pain and emptiness of their *real* lives.

Children and young adults will often create fantasies in which they become a hero or celebrity. At some point in the fantasy, they will usually win the love, adulation, and respect of their parents, friends, or peers. They may also engage in dark fantasies, where they are killing, raping, molesting, or controlling these same people. Finally, when fantasy addiction is combined with love, sex, and romance addiction, these addicts may pass their entire day creating love, sex, and romance scenes in their heads.

Fantasy addicts spend so much time obsessing over the past and dreaming about the future that they are cut off from the present. Cut off from the present, they are like people who have become lost at sea and do not have a single star to guide them.

Addiction to Physical Pain, Stress, and Rage

M any spiritually wounded people use physical pain and suf-
fering to medicate the emotional pain of their lives. A
large number of them, mostly young women, engage in a form of
self-mutilation known as "cutting." They cut themselves until
they bleed profusely, which provides for them the same sort of
mood-altering effect that a shot of booze provides an alcoholic.

Stress addicts try to distract themselves from the pain and
emptiness of their lives by rushing around trying to do too many
things at once or trying to please too many people at once.
Chronic stress leads to all sorts of painful physical symptoms such
as ulcers, headaches, and knots in your gut. Rage addicts are people who alter their moods by releasing anger in an uncontrolled
and unhealthy way, and they often physically injure themselves or
others in the process.

As we grow in our recovery, we will find that we no longer
need to physically injure ourselves to deaden the emotional pain of
our lives. Life becomes increasingly pain-free, as we begin to exist in harmony with the Tao.

Thinking Addiction

Children who are not allowed to freely express themselves, or who have suffered painful and traumatic experiences, will likely jump up into their heads. When this occurs, the seeds of thinking addiction are sown. Thinking addicts rely too much on rational thought and logic, and rely too little on their natural instincts and intuition. As a result, they take most of their guidance from the abstract world of beliefs, principles, morals, and religious doctrine, rather than from their gut feelings and their conscience.

Our educational system tends to encourage addictive thinking, as children are frequently asked to tell their teachers what they *think* about something, rather than how they truly feel. Thinking addicts often seem muddled and confused when they try to relate how they feel. This is because they are disconnected from many of their feelings, and it can take years of psychotherapy to reconnect with them.

The Taoist is guided by her natural instincts, as well as by her brain. Her thinking is clear, and her senses are razor sharp.

Addiction to Religion, Morality, Rules, and Laws

Many people use religion to cover up the pain and emptiness of their lives. Some of these addicts find religion on their own, while others were shamed into becoming believers. In addition, many other kinds of addicts will at some point switch their addiction to religion.

A lot of people, especially religious people, are addicted to morality. They place a great deal of their self-worth in the belief that they are living a "righteous" life. But just as the two opposing forces, yin and yang, arise together, morality cannot exist without its counterpart, immorality. Hence, the moral are forever creating and persecuting the immoral.

Addiction to rules and laws is also very prevalent in our society—symbolized by a legal system that has become increasingly complex and out of touch with reality. Our legal system attempts to catch the fish of truth in a complex net of laws, rules, and codes. Truth, however, is more like water than a fish; thus it cannot be apprehended in a net.

The Taoist has little use for religion, morality, rules, and laws. He is content to simply go along with the natural order of things.

The Need to Belong

C hildren need to feel that they belong somewhere. If they are unable to gain this acceptance from their families, schools, and communities, they may be drawn to one or more outside groups to meet this need. And when their desperate need for acceptance is coupled with a lot of pent-up anger, they are prone to gravitate toward hate groups and gangs.

Children who look to a group for acceptance are often quickly indoctrinated and soon begin to identify themselves completely with the group. They can also become addicted to the group and may be willing to do almost anything to maintain or improve their group status.

The Taoist does not look to any group or religion for acceptance or to define who he is. He is perfectly content with who he is, and he frequently experiences the sensation of wholeness and belonging to the world.

Addiction to Power, Wealth, Success, and Fame

A ddiction to power is perhaps the most dangerous addiction of all, since it requires the subordination of others, at best, and, at worst, has been responsible for the subjugation and even genocide of entire races of people.

Wealth addicts are people who can never possess enough money, property, stocks, and bonds. Some of them sock away their money and act as if they were paupers. Others enjoy showing off their wealth, and they purchase all sorts of expensive toys and status symbols. Since wealth addicts place much of their self-worth in their wealth, many of them live their entire lives in fear of losing it.

Those who are addicted to success and fame are usually not able to find much love from within. As a result, they seek love and adulation from the entire world.

The Taoist is content to live simply, to be unimportant, and to not lord it over others. Her only desire is to exist in harmony with the great Tao.

Addiction to Appearances and Images

Toxically shamed people tend to put a lot of their self-worth in appearances and images. One recovering addict put it best, when he said, "Pretty on the outside—ugly on the inside."

People who fit this category may be obsessed with trying to appear cool, hip, stylish, thin, pretty, handsome, cultured, spiritual, or erudite. Makeup addicts, workout addicts, anorexics, and bulimics also fall into this category, as well as those who need to show off status symbols, and those who must have a beautiful woman or a handsome man on their arm in order to feel okay.

All of this superficial behavior is a byproduct of something very deep—low self-esteem. In recovery, we learn to accept and love ourselves for who we are. Once this is achieved, we will no longer need to create an image of ourselves that is acceptable to others. We will find that our strength lies not in outward appearances, but in a feeling of deep inner peace and belonging.

The Need for Stimulation

M any spiritually wounded people need constant stimulation to help distract them from the pain and emptiness of their lives. In addition to using chemical stimulants, we can also be stimulated by, and become addicted to, gambling, working, traveling, shopping, music and partying, racing and cruising, joking and fooling around, sports and exercise, reading, movies, computers, telephones, radios, televisions, video games, holidays and events, and superficial banter and gossip.

The constant need for stimulation creates an imbalance in our lives. To achieve balance, we must learn to be comfortable with silence and solitude, and allow time each day for introspection and contemplation.

Addiction to Shopping, Junk, and Sacred Objects

People from dysfunctional upbringings tend to surround themselves with a lot of stuff. Those who are compulsive shoppers get high from the excitement of shopping and spending money. Some of them are bargain-hunters, while others will pay top dollar for fancy, new things to show off.

Other people cannot seem to throw anything away and are not comfortable unless they are surrounded by mountains of junk. Still others are obsessed with collecting "sacred objects," out of which they construct all types of shrines and altars for their "sacred services."

The Taoist owns very little. Her mind is free of clutter and so is her environment. She recognizes that the Tao runs through all things; thus she does not consider one object or place to be any more sacred than another.

Sitting on the "Pity Pot"

All recovering people go through periods where they sit on the "pity pot." This is a necessary and unavoidable stage of the recovery process. For some, however, this behavior can become addictive. When this occurs, they may be no better off than when they were using their drug of choice. They can find themselves stuck in a quagmire so deep, they may never find their way out—their spiritual journey ended.

A recovery slogan says, "If you have one foot in the past and another in the future, you shit all over today." If we continue to stay at home and feel sorry for ourselves, if we continue to look for sympathy and pity from others, if we continue to beat ourselves up, if we continue to fantasize about the way things used to be, the way things could have been, or the way things might be in the future, we will remain spiritually sick.

It's okay to sit on the "pity pot" occasionally, but at some point we need to move on with our recovery and our lives. The past is just an echo; the future is just speculation. All that really exists is the eternal Now, which the Chinese call the eternal Tao.

Addiction to Virtue

M any people spend their entire lives trying to save the environment, trying to save souls, and in general, trying to save the world. It is important to recognize that altruistic behavior, although considered virtuous by Western standards, is really an inferior form of virtue insofar as Taoism is concerned.

Te (pronounced *deh*) is a Chinese word that means virtue. Te is not virtue in the sense of going around trying to do good deeds. It is a state of being that results from living in accord with the Tao. When one attains this state, one is usually not even aware of one's virtuous acts, for these acts arise as naturally as flowers arise in springtime.

We can and must heal the planet from the damage we humans have inflicted upon her. But the best way to achieve this healing is to heal ourselves. When this occurs, Mother Earth and all of her children will once again begin to exist in harmony with the great Tao.

Addiction to Peace and Love

A lot of people tend to gravitate toward religions, spiritual communities, and healing and growth centers that speak of peace and love ad nauseam. This is a natural response by those who grew up believing in a God who was anything but loving, and by those who have experienced some degree of childhood abuse, neglect, abandonment, and shame.

Expressions such as "All is love" and "All is peace" ring hollow, as they do not reflect the way things actually exist in nature. It is like putting your faith in a one-sided coin or in a magnet that has only one pole. The harmony Lao Tzu spoke of in his *Tao Te Ching,* and the harmony I speak of in this book, includes both the soft and the hard, the violent and the serene, the strong and the weak, the wicked and the good, feelings of anger and feelings of love.

Only when we have experienced and accepted both the positive and the negative—the yin and the yang—can we truly achieve a unity with nature and thus a unity with the eternal Tao.

Denial

Most of us have the ability to see dysfunctional behavior in others, yet we often remain in denial of our own dysfunctional tendencies. The reason is that once we come out of denial, we must then begin a healing process, with all the grief, emptiness, and pain one is prone to experience in early recovery.

We must never wait for someone else to come out of denial to make the changes we need to make. If we wait for validation from parents, siblings, spouses, friends, or peers, it will only delay our recovery. We must be willing to let go of anyone or anything that stands in our way. We do not need to go it alone, however, as there are many others who have blazed this path before us, and there are many support groups to aid us in our recovery.

Once we embark on our spiritual journey, we will begin to undergo a wondrous transformation of the body-mind. In time, we will find peace within ourselves and with the world around us. When this occurs, we will have reached our "stillpoint," which is a translation of a Chinese expression that means, "our heart will be settled."

| Three |

Harmonizing Our Relationships

Harmonizing Our Relationships

The members of a family are like pieces to a puzzle. The way these pieces fit together depends upon the role or roles each individual takes on. In healthy families, the members simply *play* their roles without becoming too attached to them. In dysfunctional families, the members tend to *become* their roles. They identify themselves with, and place much of their self-worth in, their roles.

We often develop our roles at an early age, and there are many factors that go into determining them, such as birth order, sickness or death in the family, war, poverty, divorce, unemployment, and the era we grew up in. In dysfunctional families, children tend to take on roles that bring them the most attention and approval, as well as roles that allow them to simply survive.

Many of us continue to play our childhood roles throughout our lives. As a result, we often remain stuck in unhealthy and unfulfilling relationships. To move forward on our spiritual journey, we must begin to let go of these roles and focus on improving our relationship skills and building intimacy in our relationships. Once we begin this process, all of our relationships will start to become healthier and more harmonious.

Workplace Roles

It is quite common for people to engage in dysfunctional role-playing at work: Bosses often play the role of "the disappointed parent," while workers play the role of "the irresponsible child." Those who overfunctioned or underfunctioned in their childhood tend to continue this behavior throughout their working careers. Those who were forced into the role of "peacemaker" as children can find themselves compulsively settling disputes between coworkers. The family clown often becomes the office practical joker; people-pleasers may become brown-nosers; tattle-tales may become backstabbers.

Dysfunctional role-playing is not limited to the workplace, however. Such behavior is often evident in the classroom, on the playground, at religious and social functions, and even at Twelve-Step meetings.

As we start to let go of our old, familiar roles, we will begin to surround ourselves with healthier people who are committed to growing with us. As a result, our work life, our family life, and our social life will become much healthier, and our overall quality of life will greatly improve.

People Using Each Other

People who are raised in dysfunctional environments tend to use each other to try to medicate their pain. Toxically shamed children will often try to get their parents to buy them fancy things and take them to exciting places, which makes them feel okay for a while. Toxically shamed parents will often try to use their children's accomplishments to try to medicate their own pain.

Most addicts tend to surround themselves with a vast and complex network of co-addicts, each using one another to feed their own addictions. In fact, some of these addicts will try to use everyone they come into contact with—friends, siblings, lovers, coworkers, bosses, ministers, as well as perfect strangers. Using others to feed an emotional dependency is a very common and insidious form of addiction. We should always be aware of our energy level and avoid those who try to emotionally drain us. We should also make sure that *we* do not engage in this type of behavior.

The Taoist does not attempt to use others to meet an unhealthy need; nor does he allow himself to be used for such a purpose.

We Seek Those Who Reflect Our Inner Woundedness

Young children tend to gravitate toward the person or people who can best meet their needs, are the most nurturing, and can give them the most love. At some point, however, this phenomenon ends, and they begin to gravitate toward those who simply reflect their inner woundedness.

We are destined to seek out, and be attracted to, people who have the same size "hole" as us. For example, two people may look different, act different, have been raised in different socioeconomic conditions, have received different levels of education, and yet, on the inside, they can still be identical.

There is a saying in recovery, "We become one parent and marry the other." This truism explains why many of the same dysfunctional patterns continue to persist in families, generation after generation. As we begin to heal, we will be free to choose healthy individuals to be in relationship with, thus breaking the cycle of dysfunction.

People-Pleasing

People-pleasers are individuals who place a lot of their self-worth in what others think of them. Like most addicts, people-pleasers will do almost anything for a fix, and they will neglect many of their responsibilities when they are using. Ironically, while they may be so focused on getting approval from some, they tend to be quite nasty to others, especially those who get in the way of their people-pleasing.

People-pleasers are usually very unhappy for a number of reasons: They do a lot for other people, while doing very little for themselves; they are very easy to manipulate and are often taken advantage of; they frequently find themselves in situations where they have to prove themselves, yet they tend to surround themselves with people who withhold their approval.

The Taoist surrounds herself with people who love and accept her for who she is, and who do not require her to prove herself or to earn this love and acceptance. She can therefore focus on pleasing herself, and in doing so, she is able to please most everyone else.

Addictive Relationships

A relationship addict is a person who uses others to try to gain wholeness. Once this bonding, or *enmeshment,* takes place, the relationship takes on all the characteristics of a drug addiction. Since their partners become their "drugs," in order to ensure a steady supply of "fixes," they feel compelled to monitor, rescue, caretake, nag, control, manipulate, and cling to them. The goal of this behavior ranges from trying to change the person into someone they can live with, to simply trying to keep him or her alive. This kind of behavior is often called *codependency.*

Most addictive relationships are characterized by a repeating cycle of intense pleasure followed by intense pain. Only when the pain of the relationship becomes greater than the pain they are attempting to escape, are they able to end it. In some instances, a relationship becomes so hellish that the people involved look at death as their only way out. Oftentimes, when an addictive relationship does end, the withdrawal may be so intense that one or both partners immediately begins the search to find someone or something to fill the void, and in many instances the couple will reunite, with no growth having occurred.

Attempting to use others to complete ourselves is futile and only serves to keep us in a disharmonious state. As we begin to heal, we will come to recognize that we are already complete. We are already whole.

Love and Romance Addiction

Many spiritually wounded people are unable to experience feelings of love. Many others, however, not only experience these feelings, they become addicted to them. They are the love and romance addicts. Love and romance addicts live in a fantasy world. They often fantasize about rescuing a damsel in distress, being rescued by a knight in shining armor, or finding a soul mate—the one person on the planet who will make their lives complete.

Love and romance addiction is fueled by a desire to fill an empty void and is intensified by a biochemical response to certain stimuli—namely the look, feel, smell, sound, and taste of certain people. The chemicals that are automatically released in the brains of love and romance addicts produce a high that is similar to what substance abusers experience when they manually inhale, ingest, or inject their drugs.

Love and romance addicts do not have to be in a relationship to practice their addiction. Once in a romantic situation, however, they often become hooked on the other person and can suffer through a terrible withdrawal when they split up, regardless of who made the decision to leave.

The Taoist regards feelings of love as no more or less important than any other feelings he experiences. He simply experiences these feelings and then lets go of them. In this way, he remains centered in the Tao.

Sexual Addiction

There exists an entire spectrum of sexual behaviors that people can become addicted to. These behaviors range from simply talking, joking, and fantasizing about sex, to pornography, voyeurism, and masturbation, to sexual abuse, incest, and rape.

Although thinking about sex and becoming sexually aroused is perfectly normal, healthy, and natural human behavior, sex addicts will use sex in abnormal, unhealthy, and unnatural ways: They may use sex to get attention, praise, or to gain acceptance; to obtain security, money, or narcotics; or simply to get high, medicate their pain, and fill an empty void.

Sexual addiction is often combined with love and romance addiction. When this occurs, the addict tends to *objectify* just about everyone he or she meets—viewing them not as people, but merely as potential lovers or sex-mates. Another element of both sex and love addiction is *intrigue*. Intrigue means to view someone as mysterious and exotic in order to heighten the excitement. Objectification and intrigue are very superficial and are therefore the antithesis of intimacy.

Sexual urges and desires are a natural part of the human condition and should always be acknowledged. These urges do not always need to be acted upon, however, and one should never force any kind of sexual encounter. Such action can only result in extreme disharmony and resistance.

Developing Good Relationship Skills

To have healthy relationships, we must develop good relationship skills. Most of our relationship skills come from our parents. They are the models. If they have problems getting their needs met in their relationships, then we will probably encounter the same difficulties in our relationships.

Getting our needs met in our relationships is one of the ways we take care of ourselves, and learning to take care of ourselves is an important part of our recovery. Moreover, once we can take care of ourselves, we will then be better equipped to meet the needs of others.

There are four important steps to getting our needs met in our relationships: We must first *identify* our needs. Second, we must be able to *communicate* our needs in an appropriate manner. Third, we must learn to set *boundaries* around our needs. Fourth, we must be willing and able to *enforce* these boundaries. If we are unable to accomplish any one of these four steps, we may find ourselves repeatedly stuck in unfulfilling relationships.

Of course, there are many other relationship skills to work on, such as learning to negotiate, discuss, compromise, and listen. As we progress in our recovery, we will continue to improve all of our relationship skills. With our newly honed skills, our relationships and our lives will become richer and more satisfying, as we move inexorably closer to harmony with the Tao.

Healthy Ways to Communicate

Once we have identified our needs, it is vitally important to communicate them in a healthy way. It is best to communicate our needs in a calm, straightforward manner, using "I language" whenever possible. "I language" means to speak in the first person. For example, it is better to say, "I would like you to give me more affection," than to say, "You never give me affection anymore!"

When we are communicating our needs, we should speak directly to the person involved. We should also avoid arguing and fighting, or using anger, guilt, fear, and intimidation to get what we want. We should spell out exactly what we need from the other person—leaving nothing for them to have to guess or to figure out. We should also set clear and precise boundaries around our needs and be very clear about the consequences for violating these boundaries.

The Taoist has learned to skillfully communicate his needs and to set boundaries around them. He speaks softly, but firmly, for he knows that he can enforce any boundary he sets. With good relationship skills, he is able to get his needs met without a lot of effort.

When We Are Unable to Get Our Needs Met

When we are stuck in a living, working, or social situation where we are unable to get our needs met, we can become quite miserable, and we often take our misery out on those around us. We also tend to use all kinds of drugs to help numb our pain.

Sometimes we are legitimately stuck by unusual circumstances in a situation that does not meet our needs. When this occurs, we must make the most of the situation and leave as quickly as possible. Most of the time, however, we simply believe we are stuck—a belief based on false information and a fear of change. It is therefore *we* who are most often to blame for not getting our needs met.

The Taoist recognizes that she holds the key to her own happiness. She is not afraid to make changes in her life, and she can easily let go of people and situations that do not meet her needs.

Love Is Not Enough

Love is just one of many ingredients that go into making a healthy relationship. There are other elements that are equally important such as trust, communication, intimacy, and honesty; being able to give encouragement, acceptance, understanding, and validation; having similar interests, feeling comfortable with each other, and giving each other room to grow.

It is important to make sure that people can meet our needs before we begin a relationship with them. A person who is in any kind of active addiction that makes him or her physically or emotionally unavailable should be avoided. We should also avoid entering into relationships for the sake of appearances, to satisfy someone else, or simply because we found someone who likes us and will give us the attention we crave. And we should be quite wary of relationships that begin after we have "rescued" someone from a bad relationship or were "rescued" from one ourselves.

The Taoist recognizes that love is just one of many important ingredients that go into making a healthy relationship. She has identified her other needs, and she seeks those who are able and eager to meet them.

Growing Out of Relationships

As we grow in our recovery, we will have a better understanding of who we are and what we want out of life. As a result, we will begin to surround ourselves with healthier people who can meet our newly defined needs.

Although it is possible for people to grow together in a relationship, recovering people often find themselves growing apart from their families, friends, and spouses. And since recovery is an ongoing process, we will most likely continue to grow out of our relationships, including relationships with other recovering people, our sponsors, and our therapists.

We cannot force other people to grow with us, and those who try to change other people are probably stuck themselves. Conversely, people who are changing for someone else's benefit are probably not making any real growth either. Finally, those who are waiting around for another person to change are simply avoiding or delaying making the changes *they* need to make.

The Taoist recognizes that spiritual growth is an ongoing process, and that his relationships simply reflect where he is at in this process. As he continues to grow, he watches his relationships bloom and then wither away and then bloom again.

The Range of Relationships

Relationships range from very superficial to very intimate. People from dysfunctional backgrounds tend to gravitate toward the extremes. Many of them have a disproportionate number of superficial and casual relationships, while others try to be intimate with just about everyone they meet.

Healthy relationships usually begin on a superficial level and develop slowly. As two people get to know each other, they may eventually become good friends or even lovers. Sex, love, romance, and other kinds of relationship addicts are often impatient in their relationships, and they try to hurry things along. But without enough time to develop properly, a relationship can become very unhealthy.

The Taoist takes her time and allows her relationships to develop naturally. She also maintains a healthy balance in her relationships. She knows when it is appropriate to be intimate with someone, and when it is not.

Supporting Others

I t is important to learn how to support others in a healthy way. When we try to change or fix people, we are not supporting them in a healthy way. When we constantly nag people and try to control, monitor, rescue, or force our will upon them, we are not supporting them in a healthy way. When we take on other people's responsibilities and enable them to continue unhealthy behaviors and addictions, we are not supporting them in a healthy way.

The healthiest way to support others is to set a good example ourselves. We do this by taking care of our own needs and responsibilities and by modeling healthy communication and boundary-setting skills. We can also support others by being available to talk to them and to listen to them, as long as we can remain detached from any craziness they may be involved in. Most important, we can support people simply by loving and accepting them for who they are and where they are in their recovery.

By learning to support others in a healthy way, we not only maintain our own serenity, we give them an opportunity to experience serenity as well.

Authority Figures

Most people who grew up in dysfunctional environments have issues with authority figures. Some of them have it so bad, they cannot work for anyone but themselves. Others constantly argue and fight with their bosses, while at the same time seeking praise and approval from them. When this praise and approval is not forthcoming, they may become angry, depressed, and feel empty. They may also go out and use, even if they have been clean and sober for a long time.

People from dysfunctional upbringings also have a difficult time accepting criticism. They tend to take all criticism as a personal attack, and they frequently overreact and feel deeply hurt after being criticized. This is because criticism brings their toxic shame to the surface, and it stings.

We tend to be attracted to people who remind us of our original authority figures—our parents. Many of us engage in a futile attempt to re-create our childhood, and to get our needs met this time. This is why we so often find bosses, spouses, therapists, and sponsors who are enablers, will not accept us, or are emotionally or physically abusive toward us.

As we continue to grow and heal, we will be able to distinguish between those in authority who are abusing their power and those who are simply doing their jobs. We will find a boss who meets our needs as a boss, not as a father. We will find a spouse who meets our needs as a spouse, not as a mother.

Trying to Make Relationships Work

An old recovery slogan says, "It is much easier to put on slippers than to try to carpet the whole world." This is especially true for relationships. It is much easier to simply leave a relationship than to try to change everything about a person or an organization.

Contrary to popular belief, we do not have to work hard to have healthy relationships. Healthy relationships happen naturally and do not require a lot of effort to sustain. We must examine our core issues to determine why we are willing to try so hard in our relationships, and why we often feel so stuck in them. We will likely determine that abandonment issues, flawed beliefs, and poor relationship skills are the driving force behind much of this effort.

Trying to make relationships work requires a lot of effort and often yields few results. Such behavior is tantamount to swimming against the current, which will quickly sap our strength and energy.

Controlling and Abusive Relationships

M any relationship addicts are jealous, untrusting, possessive, and controlling, and they often monitor, spy upon, and even stalk their partners. In addition, they frequently use anger, guilt, fear, intimidation, and physical violence to get what they want. On the other hand, these same people may also allow *themselves* to be controlled and abused, rather than risk a breakup of the relationship.

There are many reasons why people remain stuck in controlling and abusive relationships: They are re-creating their dysfunctional childhood environment; they are afraid to ask for help or to make a change; they are overly dependent upon the other person.

Controlling and abusive behavior is one of the hallmarks of an addictive relationship. To break the cycle of addictive relationships, we must continue to challenge our beliefs, work on our core issues, and develop healthy relationship skills. As a result, our relationships will become much more comfortable and serene.

Searching for the Perfect Person

Some of us spend our entire lives searching for the perfect person—the one who will make us feel whole and complete. This is because our society, our peers, our family, and our religion often try to make us feel incomplete when we are without a significant other.

Those who desperately seek a man or a woman to complete them will probably be unhappy even if they do find someone to bond with. For just as someone's extreme hunger will prevent him or her from finding food, an extreme need to be in a relationship can prevent us from finding healthy people to be in relationship with.

It is important to enter into a new relationship from a position of wholeness. To do this, we must change some of our core beliefs. The most important belief to change is, "I will not be okay until I find that one, right person—my soul mate."

The Taoist is not looking for someone to complete him. He knows that he is okay whether he is romantically involved or not. He is therefore able to enter into new relationships from a state of wholeness.

Identity and Enmeshment

A common characteristic of many dysfunctional relationships is *enmeshment*. When two or more people become enmeshed, the identity of each becomes blurred. Our identity is who we really are, which is the sum total of our feelings and experiences, our likes and needs, our strengths and weaknesses, our hopes and dreams.

When we become enmeshed with other people, we tend to take on their pain and sorrow, adopt their dreams, and cater to their needs and tastes. As a result, we go through life without knowing who *we* really are and what *we* really want.

As we continue on our journey to wholeness, we will start to disentangle ourselves from other people and begin to figure out who we really are. We will let go of unhealthy relationships, and we will often be alone. When we can be alone without feeling lonely, we are then primed to experience the great Tao.

Being Vulnerable

M any of us learned early in life not to allow ourselves to be vulnerable. We constructed a hard shell around us—a thick, impenetrable wall, complete with armed guards—to turn away those who attempt to get close. Although this wall may have helped us when were growing up, fearing and avoiding intimacy makes it difficult for us to have fulfilling relationships today.

Occasionally, we may come out of our shells and become intimate with someone. But without the necessary tools to have healthy relationships, the experience is usually painful. Afterward, we may go right back into our shells. We may come to the erroneous conclusion that all men or all women cannot be trusted, and we might swear off close relationships forever. What we failed to realize was that it was our selection of people and our weak relationship skills that were to blame. We must therefore continue to work on our core issues, hone our relationship skills, and try it again.

The Taoist allows people to get close to her. She recognizes that such vulnerability may cause her occasional pain, but that this pain is far less than the pain of a lonely and empty life.

Intimacy

To be intimate means to share our private feelings and experiences with someone. It means to be completely honest, trusting, and open. It means to be vulnerable. Those who have a problem being intimate need to determine which of their core issues are responsible. People with serious abandonment issues or who were abused as children may need to be treated by a psychotherapist before they can enjoy intimate relationships.

To achieve intimacy with others, we must first achieve intimacy with ourselves: We must reconnect to our feelings and experiences and fully embrace the wounded child within us; we must identify our needs, our likes, and our dreams; we must be completely honest with ourselves and begin to love and accept ourselves unconditionally.

The Taoist has nothing to hide. He is completely honest with himself and others, and he is not afraid to be vulnerable. Being intimate with himself and others, he achieves balance and harmony in his relationships.

| Four |

Learning to Go with the Flow

Learning to Go with the Flow

Many of us have been going against the flow of nature for much of our lives. In order to grow and heal, we must begin the slow process of turning our ship around so that we are going *with* the flow. To do this, we must transcend our own nature and go against our own grain. We must learn to take risks and do things that are new, strange, and make us feel uncomfortable.

Over time, we will be able to let go of many of the roles and behaviors that allowed us to survive when we were growing up, but that no longer serve us. We will also start releasing our toxic shame and begin to experience periods of serenity, with all of the inner peace, joy, and wholeness this brings. For we will have turned our ship around and begun to go along with the flow of the great Tao.

No Recipe for Recovery

"The Tao that can be told is not the eternal Tao." These famous words from Lao Tzu's *Tao Te Ching* point out that there is no way to teach Tao. There is no recipe for it—no A, B, C, D to follow that will show us how to get from where we are now to a state of blissful oneness with all things. The best Lao Tzu could do was to point the way. He could tell us *what* to do, but not *how* to do it.

There is no recipe for recovery, either. There are the Twelve Steps, but they merely point the way. They tell us *what* to do, but not *how* to do it. Receiving psychotherapy, attending meetings, seminars, and workshops, reading books and listening to tapes, all play a role in the healing process. Yet, some of us do all of this and seem to get nowhere, while others appear to do very little, but they progress much more rapidly. This then begs the question, How does one recover?

Creating Balance in Our Lives

C reating balance in our lives is one of the most important facets of the recovery process. We need to become aware of the areas in our lives that are out of balance and begin to correct them. For example, if we are too self-reliant, we should learn to rely more on others. If we are overly dependent on others, we should learn to do some things on our own. If we act too impulsively, we need to learn to become more disciplined. If we have too much self-control, we need to learn to become more spontaneous.

Some of us work too much, while others will do anything to get out of working. It is important to balance work with play, seriousness with lightheartedness, exercise with rest, being alone with being with others, speaking with listening, noisiness with silence, activity with stillness.

The Taoist is aware of the areas in his life that are out of balance, and he strives to correct them. In this way, he achieves harmony between yin and yang.

Creating a Healing Balance

When our body suffers a deep wound, we know that we must do something to help ourselves heal. If we do not do anything, the wound is likely to become infected. But once we have cleaned and dressed the wound, we must then allow nature to take over and finish the job.

The same holds true for our psychospiritual wounds. We must do something to help ourselves heal, but we must not do too much. We can read recovery literature, join a support group, receive psychotherapy, attend seminars and workshops; but then we must *stop* doing and allow nature to take over. If we are constantly trying to heal these wounds ourselves, we impede nature's ability to heal us. This is especially true for those Twelve-Steppers who are constantly working the Steps and not allowing their "higher power" to be part of the healing process.

The Taoist knows what things she can do to help heal her childhood wounds. She is then able to let go and allow nature to finish the job. By creating a healing balance, she heals quickly.

Working Through the Pain

P art of the healing process involves reconnecting to feelings and events that were so painful, we either consciously suppressed them or unconsciously dissociated from them. This can be a very emotional and painful process, but is absolutely essential if we are to heal. Moreover, until we are able to own our childhood pain and sorrow, we will continue to relive it. The good news is that every time we are able to put an old issue to rest, we will make an important growth step, and we will carry around less pain.

It is important to point out that there is usually some pain involved when we meet an important need for the first time. For instance, those who have never been hugged and told how special they are may experience some degree of pain when this finally does occur. This pain will begin to subside, however, once the need is consistently met.

Our journey to wholeness can be painful at times. It is important to embrace and to own our pain and to feel the feelings we hid from for so many years. The pain will decrease as we begin to work through it, and our lives will become healthier and more joyful.

Reparenting Ourselves

M ost of the dysfunction in our lives can be traced to basic childhood needs that were not properly met. In recovery, we become our own loving parents. We learn to love and accept ourselves unconditionally. We learn to meet our present needs and to address our old issues.

When we have identified and are starting to work on our core issues, it is wise to be in the care of a competent psychothera-pist and to have a network of supportive people around, as some deep wounds are likely to open up. Even after we have worked on our issues for a long time, we may still have problems in certain areas. But it is important to remember that recovery is about "progress—not perfection."

The process of reparenting ourselves can be long and pain-ful, but the rewards are great. In time, the pain will subside and will be replaced by a feeling of wholeness and serenity.

Taking Charge of Our Lives

As we continue to grow in our recovery, we will learn to take charge of our lives. We will begin to make positive changes and to take risks. We will stop playing the role of a victim. We will become *actors,* rather than *reactors.*

Actors are active participants in life, whereas reactors tend to view life from the sidelines. Actors are able to let go of unhealthy situations and do not try to change other people. Reactors tend to wait around for other people to change or for some kind of windfall to save them from their unhappiness. Actors own their feelings: When they become angry, they simply say, "I am angry." They do not say, "You are making me angry," as reactors are prone to say. Actors communicate their needs and set healthy boundaries. Reactors let people step all over them and always seem to be waiting for the next shoe to drop...on them.

The Taoist takes charge of his life and does not blame others for his misfortunes. He is accountable for his own actions and is responsible for his own happiness.

Keeping Our Power

When we look to an external source to relieve our pain and emptiness, we tend to give our power over to that source. It is like striking a deal with the devil, for once we hand our personal power over to this external source, it then controls our destiny. Our lives go up and down like a roller coaster ride, as we go through our daily highs and lows.

Relationship addicts give their partners a lot of power by being dependent upon them. People-pleasers give their power away to those they seek to impress. Substance abusers give up their power to their drugs, suppliers, and enablers.

The Taoist does not give away his personal power to people, places, and things. As a result, his life runs smooth and steady. Such attainment is called "finding the Middle Way."

Substituting Healthy Activities

Human beings are creatures of habit. We must therefore substitute healthy activities for any unhealthy behaviors we are accustomed to engaging in. We especially should avoid *idle time* whenever possible. Many recovering people refer to idle time as "the devil's workplace."

Examples of healthy activities are building and gardening, cooking and cleaning, sports and exercise, singing and dancing, playing and having fun, attending recovery meetings and seminars, reading and writing, sitting quietly and meditating. It is important to point out that quiet time differs from idle time, in that the former promotes healing, growth, and balance, whereas the latter encourages stagnation, boredom, and "stinking thinking."

The Taoist fills her day with healthy activities. With a balanced and disciplined lifestyle, she avoids idle time and all of the problems it can create.

Working Through the Cravings

As recovering people, we often experience strong cravings to go back to old habits and relationships. When these cravings occur, we have three choices: We can give in to them; we can stuff them; or we can work through them.

The first choice, giving in to our cravings, doesn't work, because, as every recovering addict knows, "One is too many, and a thousand is never enough." The second choice, stuffing the feelings, doesn't work either, because any part of us we do not accept and own has a way of owning *us*. It is much better to keep the urges and cravings in front of us. We need to look at them, feel them, and work through them, without acting upon them.

The Taoist acknowledges and works through any unhealthy urges and cravings he experiences. In this way, he does not give them any power.

The Process of Letting Go

There is often a long process we must go through before we can let go of an unhealthy relationship, situation, or substance. During this process, we will go through many of the same stages we would go through if we were facing our own death. In a sense, part of us *is* dying, and we are afraid. We are afraid of what our lives might be like without this person, place, or thing. We are afraid we might not survive.

The process of letting go is often divided into high periods and low periods. The high periods, which recovering people call "pink-clouding," usually do not last as long as the low periods. During a low period, it is easy to become mired in self-pity, and it is helpful to have supportive people around to help us get through it. When we finally do begin to pull out of it, we will have reached some degree of acceptance and closure, and we will be able to move on with our lives.

Over time, it becomes increasingly easier to let go of people, places, and substances that do not serve us. We know things will turn out all right. We know we will live through it. Each time we let go of an unhealthy part of our lives, we move one step closer to wholeness and harmony.

Anger

Anger is a natural boundary and is part of the wide spectrum of feelings we are prone to experience. Most people who had dysfunctional upbringings have various problems and issues around anger. These people can be divided into two categories: those who get angry too much, and those who are unable to get angry at all. Both groups can benefit greatly from some form of anger therapy.

When children are not allowed to freely express their anger, they are forced to stuff these feelings. When the anger finally does come out, it can take the form of a destructive and uncontrolled rage, or it can be released slowly in a series of passive-aggressive acts, which can be just as hurtful and destructive. Holding in anger can also result in a host of physical and emotional symptoms.

A lot of our anger comes from the inability to get our needs met. This anger will start to dissipate as we improve our relationship skills and learn to take care of ourselves. Another source of anger is fear—fear of abandonment, fear of making a mistake, fear of living without someone or something we have become dependent upon. As we continue to work on our core issues, much of our fear-based anger will also begin to dissipate.

The Taoist acknowledges anger whenever it arises. He then releases it in an appropriate manner. In this way, he avoids carrying it around and becoming its prisoner.

Grief

Grieving is a necessary part of the healing process. But just as there are people who are unable to get angry, there are those who are unable to grieve. One of the main symptoms of unexpressed grief is a chronic low-grade depression. People who suffer from this tend to use a wide variety of stimulants just to make it through the day. Many of them become hooked on these stimulants and believe they could not survive without them.

It is important to reconnect with our past and begin the grieving process. A competent psychotherapist may be required to prime the pump and start the tears flowing. It is wise to come off as many of our drugs as possible at this time, so we will be able to feel all of our feelings.

If we have a lot of unexpressed grief, we may find ourselves consumed with grief at the breakup of a relationship, the loss of a pet, or some other natural event. These events are triggering the release of a lifetime of unexpressed grief, pain, and sorrow. Once we become caught up, or current, in our grieving, our grieving process will become much easier and short-lived.

Grieving is an essential part of the healing process. Grieving allows us to let go of the past. Letting go of the past, we are free to live healthier, more spiritual lives in the present.

Depression

Depression is a natural part of the letting go process and is therefore necessary for healing and growth to occur. Many of us, however, suffer from a chronic low-grade depression as a result of our childhood. Much of this depression can be attributed to unexpressed anger and grief, as well as feeling stuck and powerless in our relationships, our jobs, and our lives.

A great number of us try to medicate our depression with our drugs of choice, including a wide variety of prescribed antidepressants. Unfortunately, these substances only serve to alter our present mood and do not address the causes of our depression. In order to root out these causes, we must get in touch with our anger and our grief. We must also begin to take charge of our lives and learn how to get our needs met. It is also important to refrain from using mood-altering drugs and learn to work through our depression.[1]

The Taoist recognizes that depression is a natural part of the growth process. By working through these low periods, he is able to get beyond his depression and move forward on his path to healing and harmony.

---

[1] One should always be under the supervision of one's physician or psychiatrist when attempting to come off a prescribed antidepressant.

Forgiveness, Gratitude, and Humility

As we continue along the recovery road, we begin to experience feelings of forgiveness, gratitude, and humility. We forgive others and we forgive ourselves. We even forgive God. We feel a lot of gratitude for the inner peace and serenity we now have in our lives. We are also humbled by the knowledge that we and everyone else were powerless over our past behaviors.

To reach the point of forgiveness is a process that can be very emotional and painful. Some of us make the mistake of forgiving people too soon. This may not be true forgiveness if we are trying to avoid the pain and grief of coming to terms with our issues with those people and the potential bad scene when we confront them. To let go of the past, we must first own the past.

The Taoist can forgive others for their past mistakes and abuses because she forgives herself. She is humbled by recovery and is full of gratitude for the few possessions she has and for the harmony and serenity she now experiences.

Letting Go of Our Parents

To move forward in our recovery, we need to let go of the past. We do this by healing our childhood wounds and by letting go of our parents.

We may be aware that one of our parents was dysfunctional—usually because the dysfunction was overt, and we remember it well. In recovery, we learn that both parents may have been dysfunctional—that the so-called "good" parent may have contributed just as much to the overall dysfunction of the family as the so-called "bad" parent.

It is counterproductive to sanctify one parent and vilify the other. When we categorize our parents as either "saints" or "sinners," we avoid seeing their imperfections and shortcomings, and how they were passed on to us. We also tend to carry their sorrow and pain, which can be an enormous burden. As we begin to address our issues with our parents, we will stop carrying their pain, and eventually we will be able to forgive them, and ultimately let them go.

The Taoist does not carry around any baggage from the past. He has let go of his parents, dealt with his issues, and has moved on. Thus, he is free to enjoy life in the here and now.

Taking Care of Ourselves

Recovery is the process of going from self-hatred to self-love. During this process, we stop abusing and neglecting ourselves and begin to take care of ourselves: We treat long-standing illnesses and injuries, upgrade our living and working conditions, simplify our lives, eat healthfully, get enough sleep, exercise, and relaxation, and start having some fun. We even pamper ourselves occasionally.

At some point in our recovery, we may have to say goodbye to our family of origin if they are unable to meet our newly defined needs. We will replace them with a new family of choice, who can better love, accept, trust, nurture, and validate us.

We do these things because we are worth it, and we know it! We look better, we feel better, and we enjoy life more. The pattern of self-abuse and self-neglect that began in childhood is now being replaced by love and more love.

The Taoist knows how to take care of herself. She recognizes that by taking care of herself, she is loving herself. Loving herself, she is loving the entire universe. Loving the universe, she is at one with it.

Reaping What We Sow

When we are engaged in an active addiction, our main concern is for immediate self-gratification. As a result, we often neglect our health, our job, and our family.

Even after we have sobered up, we may still have a difficult time making changes that will not bear fruit for many days, weeks, or months; thus we may see very little progress in the overall quality of our life. Since we reap what we sow, we must develop the discipline to get beyond immediate self-gratification and move toward more goal-oriented behaviors such as going back to school, taking parenting classes, joining a health club, or enrolling in a job training program.

The Taoist has the discipline to plan ahead for the future. Although he may not see the results for a long time, he knows he will eventually reap the rewards for his patience and hard work.

Relapses

Falling off the wagon is a natural part of the recovery process. In fact, it often takes a major relapse to propel us to the next level of recovery. Once we hit bottom, we can then see the entire downhill spiral and make the necessary lifestyle changes to try to prevent long, painful backslides in the future. As we progress in our recovery, we will not allow ourselves to backslide as far, and our worst bottoms will still be better than our lives were prior to recovery.

A relapse is likely to occur if we allow ourselves to become too hungry, angry, lonely, or tired. In recovery circles this is called the HALT syndrome. I actually prefer to call it the HATE syndrome—hungry, angry, tired, and empty—because when we feel empty, we will do anything to fill the void, and we usually feel a lot of self-hatred during this time. In addition to HALT and HATE, any set of adverse or unusual circumstances can send us into a relapse.

It is much better to be recovering and not clean than to be clean and not recovering. Recovering people are dealing with issues so sensitive and deeply rooted that relapses are inevitable. But each time we hit bottom, we have an opportunity to grow and to reach new spiritual heights.

Weakness and Strength

All of us have moments of great weakness, as well as periods when we are quite strong. It is important that we take steps to enhance our recovery when we are strong to minimize the potential for trouble when we go through our inevitable weak periods.

Times of weakness usually occur around the holidays, when we are sick or injured, when we are unemployed, when we are leaving a relationship, when someone close to us dies, when we are dealing with a core issue, and when we are confronted with our drug of choice. During these periods, we may have a lot of idle time, and we also tend to experience much more neediness, pain, and emptiness than at other times. With a little discipline, we can get through these weak periods without a lot of damage. We can phone a friend, keep going to meetings, try to maintain a balanced and active schedule, and try to have fun.

When we are feeling strong, we must take measures to remove our drug of choice from our lives, avoid "slippery" people, places, and things, and get rid of our "reservations"—our "dirty" phone numbers and stashes.

The Taoist recognizes that there are times when he is strong and times when he is weak. He uses self-discipline to take advantage of strong periods and to help him get past the rough times; thus he does not stray very far from the center.

Just Don't Use

In the final analysis, the only way to break a dependency is to simply not use. We must learn to take it one day at a time, one hour at a time, one minute at a time. We should also take steps to avoid our drugs whenever possible and to detach from them when we cannot avoid them.

In Alcoholics Anonymous they say, "Don't think; don't drink." Thinking leads to obsession; obsession leads to compulsion; compulsion leads to relapse. If we do find ourselves in an obsessive and compulsive mode, however, we *should* think about the consequences of our actions. We should also try to remember what our life was like the last time we gave in to the urge and used our drug of choice. Have we improved our life since? Those who still cannot stand themselves and their lives will simply not care about the consequences of using.

The Taoist allows the urge to use to flow through her and does not act upon it. She loves herself and her life, and she would not want to risk harming either.

Growth Is Slow, but Steady

Spiritual growth is a slow, but steady process. We may occasionally make a quantum leap, but for the most part we move forward by making small growth steps.

Regardless of where we are on our spiritual journey, it is important to love and accept ourselves right now. Even if we are in a relapse, or just came out of one, we should go easy on ourselves. We should never beat ourselves up.

As we move steadily forward in our recovery, the quality of our lives will continue to improve, and we will move inexorably closer to harmony with the great Tao.

Fake It 'til You Make It

Most toxically shamed people do not believe they deserve to be happy, and they tend to sabotage many of the good things in their lives. It is important to tell ourselves that we *are* worthy of happiness, even if we don't yet believe it. In recovery, this is called "fakin' it 'til you're makin' it."

The most common way to fake it 'til you make it is through the use of positive affirmations. A positive affirmation is a way of affirming, or reinforcing, a healthy and constructive belief or feeling about ourselves that we may not yet believe or feel. Here are a few examples of positive affirmations: "I am okay." "I love myself." "I don't need to have a significant other to be okay." "I am worthy." "I deserve good things in my life." "I deserve compliments and pats on the back." "I deserve to be happy."

It is important to visualize where we want to be on our spiritual journey and to head toward this destination. Although we may have to fake it at first, over time, the love we will feel for the world and for ourselves will be real, and we will no longer need to fake it. When this occurs, we will be able to enjoy our remaining days and years in unity with the great Tao.

"Follow Your Bliss"

B efore he passed on, Joseph Campbell was asked for any advice he might be willing to impart to the world. The advice he gave was, "Follow your bliss." This sage advice is easier said than done, however. For we must first discover who we are. We must then figure out what makes us happy. Finally, we must do whatever it takes to be happy.

If we remain stuck in our childhood roles and reactions, we may never figure out who we really are or what we really want out of life. If we know what we want, but still do not feel we deserve to be happy, we will also have a difficult time following Campbell's advice.

There are many among us who *have* succeeded in following their bliss. These happy, healthy, fully functioning people come in all sizes, shapes, and colors. They can be found working in a high tech research environment or in a car wash, residing in a large city or out in the country. These individuals are living up to their spiritual potential in harmony with the Tao.

Challenging the Negative Voices

M any of us have a "shitty committee" inside our heads—a chorus of voices that reinforce negative thinking and negative behavior patterns. As we grow in our recovery, we will begin to challenge these negative voices and override them with positive thoughts and affirmations. Eventually, these voices will begin to fade and will be replaced by more loving and nurturing voices.

The voices that make up our shitty committee are generally those of our parents, teachers, siblings, and other influential people from our childhood. Many of us have spent our entire lives following these voices or rebelling against them. In either case, we were cut off from our *own* feelings, needs, desires, and goals. By challenging these negative voices, we are taking a big step toward discovering who we are, and thus a big step toward following our bliss.

The Taoist has transcended the negative voices in his head. He hears them, but only laughs and pays them no mind. He now takes his direction from a much more nurturing source—the Mother of the Ten Thousand Things—the eternal Tao.

Challenging Our Beliefs

The more dysfunctional our upbringing, the more our beliefs tend to be out-of-sync with reality. It is important to challenge all of our beliefs. We must determine where they came from, and then look at them again in the new light of our recovery.

Many of our beliefs came from mom and dad. Others came from relatives, teachers, ministers, friends, and peers. Here are some examples of beliefs that need to be challenged: "Children are meant to be seen, but not heard." "My parents are saints; I'm the one who's screwed up." "Hitting my kid is okay, because my parents hit me, and I turned out all right." "I'm a bad person." "I don't deserve anything nice in my life." "This is a dog-eat-dog world, and no one will help me if I'm in trouble." "I can't make it on my own." "Everyone's out to screw me."

The Taoist continuously challenges and updates her beliefs. She keeps those that make sense to her and lets go of those that do not. By not clinging to her beliefs, she remains open to what *is*.

Reconnecting with Our Divine Inner Child

To truly follow our bliss, we need to reconnect with our divine inner child. For many of us, this can be a long and arduous process. Our inner child has gone into hiding, and it may take years of healing for him or her to trust enough to peak out. Such trust between inner child and adult is fostered through self-love and self-nurturing.

When we finally do hear the faint voice of our inner child, we must pay attention to it. As we grow in our recovery, this quiet voice will become increasingly louder, and we will find it difficult to ignore. Eventually, we will be able to reclaim much of our lost childhood. We will be able to laugh, play, and have fun—maybe for the first time ever. We will have reconnected with the part of us that is eternally young and joyous, the part of us that is at play with the entire universe, the part of us that is at one with the great Tao.

Losing Self-Consciousness

Once our inner child has come out of hiding and become part of our everyday lives, the burdensome chains of self-consciousness will begin to loosen their grip. No more will we be so concerned with how we look, speak, and act. We will become more childlike—acting spontaneously—and not worrying about how others view us. At times, we will act so naturally and spontaneously, we may completely lose track of how we are supposed to behave.

Although we will probably never lose all self-consciousness, it is important to love and accept ourselves the way we are. For despite our imperfections, the Tao will always complete us.

Serenity

As we continue on our spiritual journey, we will begin to experience moments of serenity. At first, these experiences will be fleeting, but as we progress in our recovery, they will occur more often and last longer.

We can achieve serenity at any time, but we usually experience it when our mind is clear, and we are not feeling empty or needy. It is important to emphasize that serenity cannot be achieved on demand; nor can it be held on to once we have experienced it. It is like smoke or water, and the moment we try to grab on to it, it quickly disappears.

Once we begin to experience serenity, we will have achieved a great milestone in our recovery. We will know beyond a shadow of a doubt that we have turned our ship around and are now going *with* the flow of the great Tao.

| Five |

Living the Tao

Living the Tao

This chapter is a tribute to two of the most influential people in my life: my teacher, Gia-fu Feng, and his longtime friend, Alan Watts. Gia-fu Feng directed the Stillpoint Taoist Hermitage and is best known for his and Jane English's wonderful translation of the *Tao Te Ching*. Alan Watts was a well-known philosopher, author, and teacher of Eastern thought.

Watts often remarked that to truly understand something, we must delve deeper and deeper into it. In recovery, for instance, we learn early on that we should love ourselves, but it usually takes years to truly understand and practice self-love. As we continue to hone our recovery skills, we will take our recovery to the very highest levels—and begin to live the Tao.

Raising Awareness and Sensitivity

As we continue to grow spiritually, we will become much more aware of what we say and do and become more sensitive to the needs of those around us. We will speak more softly, walk more softly, and have fewer accidents. We will also become much more aware of, and sensitive to, our natural environment, and we will learn to tread lightly there as well.

Once we begin to raise our awareness and sensitivity, we will no longer find ourselves rushing through life trying to go places or to get things accomplished. The world will begin to slow down, and we will become mindful of each precious moment.

We Cannot Deviate from the Tao

There is an old Taoist maxim that states, "The Tao is that from which one cannot deviate; that from which one *can* deviate is not the Tao." The first part of the maxim is saying that we cannot escape from the Tao, or natural process, because we are part and parcel of it. Many of us attempt to live our lives outside of the natural process, but this is as futile as trying to block out the sunlight by placing our hands over our eyes. The sun is still shining, and the Tao is still running through us, even though we may choose to believe otherwise.

The second part of this maxim says that we *can* deviate from religious doctrine and dogma, we *can* break the law, we *can* grow tired of and change our personal convictions, beliefs, opinions, and philosophies, and we *can* disobey all of the accepted rules of social conduct that form the moral framework of our particular culture. We can do all of this, because it is not the ubiquitous and eternal Tao from which we deviate, but rather the temporal and abstract world of human beings.

Singleness of Purpose

It is important to be really focused on what we are doing, no matter how minor or trivial the act may seem. To maintain such a singleness of purpose, each act must be performed with a still and open mind. We must not be easily distracted. We must be completely in the here and now.

In Zen it is said, "If you are sitting, just sit. If you are eating, just eat. If you are playing, just play." When we are completely focused on what we are doing, we are going along with the flow of the Tao; thus we have the strength of the river behind us.

"No Pick and Choose"

"No pick and choose" was a common admonition from my teacher, Gia-fu Feng, to his students. He usually said this when one of his students talked about how they *should* feel about something, rather than how they actually felt.

Many of us have decided that it is wrong to feel emotions such as anger, hatred, jealousy, and lust, and we try to disown these feelings. By picking and choosing our feelings, we are attempting to exist outside of the natural process, and thus we are cutting ourselves off from what truly *is*.

"No pick and choose" goes hand in hand with another Fengism, "Turn off your computer." Gia-fu was always telling his students to turn off their computers when they were in their heads too much and had therefore lost touch with reality.

The Taoist does not pick and choose his feelings. He simply allows them to pass through him without judgment. In this way, he harmonizes with the natural process.

Wu Wei

*W*u wei (pronounced *woo way*) is a Taoist principle that means to *not force*. Forcing almost always results in some degree of stress, tension, anger, and confrontation. And when we are all done forcing and controlling, things tend to go back to the state they were in before we unnaturally intervened.

There are several reasons why we try to force. The most common reason is a lack of skill. The more skillful we become at something, the more we tend to work *with* the natural order of things, and the less need there is to force. We also try to force when we are angry and stressed out, which often creates even more anger and stress. Another reason is lack of patience. Once we stop looking for results and stop putting in so much extra effort, things will start to fall into place naturally. Finally, we tend to force out of desire. Most desire arises from neediness, and most neediness arises from our inner woundedness. As we continue to grow and heal, we will not be so needy, and we will stop trying to force our will upon others.

The Taoist has learned to skillfully go along with the flow of natural phenomena. She has few desires. She has few needs. By not interfering with the natural process, she becomes one with it.

Who Am I?

One of the most basic philosophical questions is, Who am I? I have already stated that who I am is the sum total of my feelings and experiences, my hopes and dreams, my likes and dislikes. In fact, who I am includes all of the processes that occur within the confines of my skin, as well as all of the processes that make up my external environment.

It may be concluded from the above that we are part and parcel of the entire universal process—all that there is, and all that there ever was. Unfortunately, most of us have been taught to regard ourselves as something distinct and separate from the external world. As Alan Watts put it, "We think of ourselves as an isolated ego, or center of consciousness, locked up in a bag of skin."

Once we begin to understand who we really are, behind the ego, we will then begin to experience an indescribable feeling of harmony and wholeness. For we will be at one with the great Tao.

Spontaneous Processes

I have just stated that who I am includes all of the processes that occur both inside and outside my skin. Most of these processes are *spontaneous*—they happen by and of themselves. Whenever we try to force a spontaneous process to happen, we create all sorts of stresses and tensions, and we can even block the process from occurring at all.

Thinking is a spontaneous process. When we try to come up with an answer to a problem by scratching our head and screwing up our face, we can create a blockage that prevents us from achieving the answer we want. Falling asleep is also a spontaneous process. When we try to fall asleep, we are frequently unable. If we try to heal our childhood wounds ourselves, we do not allow nature to do its thing, and we can greatly slow down our recovery. If we try to listen, we will only tighten up the muscles around our jaw, and we will not be able to hear any better than if we simply relaxed. If we try to block certain feelings from coming up by tightening various muscles in our face and abdomen, we can give ourselves an ulcer or a headache.

The Taoist does not attempt to force or control spontaneous processes. She remains relaxed and supple and allows the universe to simply happen.

Transcending the Ego

A lan Watts defined the ego as "the marriage of a muscular strain to an illusion." I have just described the muscular strain that results from trying to control spontaneous processes such as hearing, thinking, and feeling. The illusion Watts refers to is the sensation of being separated from the world by a "bag of skin."

Many of us define ourselves by our beliefs, convictions, principles, opinions, religion, station in life, and ethnic heritage. We may also create images that make us feel better about ourselves such as "tough," "cool," "sophisticated," "spiritual," "erudite." Together, these images and abstractions form the illusion of "self."

We cannot totally get rid of our ego, but as we continue to grow and heal, we will no longer need to define ourselves with abstractions and images, and we will stop trying to control natural processes, over which we have no control. Ultimately, we will begin to transcend the ego, at which point we will experience the sensation of oneness with the entire universe.

Giving Up Attachments

G iving up attachments does not mean to disregard or dissociate from the feelings, pains, and pleasures that arise from having a body. On the contrary, it means to totally immerse ourselves in them. But once we have had these experiences, we must then let them go, so that they can come back again.

Clinging to the abstract world of religions, beliefs, and principles; clinging to unhealthy relationships, substances, and behaviors; clinging to our wealth, power, and status, only serves to weigh us down and prevents us from attaining a high level of spiritual growth.

The Taoist remains unattached to all things, yet he is living life to the fullest. He does not try to hold on to anything, because he realizes there is nothing to hold on to. The entire universe is fluid. Nothing is permanent. Everything blooms and then withers away. Everything comes into being and then returns back to the Source.

Empty Vessel

A cup that is full of sand has no room for water. When we overload the senses, we miss many of life's subtle sounds, colors, flavors, and aromas. When we overload the body, we become heavy and sluggish. When we overload the brain, we leave no room for "truth" to enter.

The Taoist has given up her attachments. She is like an empty vessel. Empty of self, she is filled by the great Tao.

Transcending the World of Symbols

Many of us tend to confuse the abstract world of signs and symbols with the things they are meant to represent. For example, we confuse ticking time—watches, clocks, and calendars—with real time, which flows on and on as eternal Now. The lines on a map are as abstract as the number five, yet some people are willing to fight and die for these lines. There are also many people who feel that the record of what has happened is more real and more important than what has actually happened.

Our legal system attempts to impose order on society with its myriad and abstract laws. We rely on lawyers to interpret these laws, and they have always found ways to wangle around them. The early Taoist sages frowned when the ancient rulers began carving their laws into stone. They knew that the true law resides in the human heart. Finally, Lao Tzu said, "The five colors blind the eyes; the five tones deafen the ears." The universe is an endless continuum of sounds, colors, and shapes. If we believe there are only five colors, we are blind to the vast array of colors in nature. If we believe there are only five tones, we are deaf to the vast array of sounds.

The Taoist experiences reality through all of her senses. She does not confuse the real world with the abstract world of signs and symbols.

Purposelessness

From our earliest days, we were taught that life had a serious purpose: School was serious; work was serious; marriage was serious; and God, with all his laws and commandments, was very serious. We were told to make something out of ourselves; to get somewhere in life; to become somebody.

Although it is important to take our adult responsibilities seriously, it is equally important to recognize that underneath it all, things are not that serious. The universe has no serious purpose. It is nonsensical—even playful. From tiny electrons to giant stars, the entire universe goes round and round—spinning, twirling, rotating, revolving—like a cosmic playground.

The Taoist wanders along the road, not going anywhere in particular, kicking rocks and tapping a stick on the ground. He realizes his life is no more serious than a cloud passing overhead or a leaf dropping from a tree. He has discovered purposelessness and will live out his days in unity with the great Tao.

Wisdom and Serenity Cannot Be Copied

For many years, I tried to imitate my teacher, Gia-fu Feng. I dressed like him, talked like him, walked like him, and tried to model my life after him in many other ways. I never could copy his wisdom and serenity, however. Once I stopped trying to imitate Gia-fu, I did eventually become more like him. By loving, nurturing, and embracing me, I have achieved within myself the wisdom and serenity I had tried for so long and so unsuccessfully to gain through external means.

The Taoist recognizes that she cannot gain inner peace and wisdom simply by reading, praying, obeying laws and commandments, or by imitating someone else. By following the Tao, she overflows with inner peace and serenity, and she possesses the wisdom of the ages.

Fear of Death

T hose who fear death tend to have a lot of attachments, and they are often obsessed with leaving their mark on society. An old Chinese proverb says, "He who is at one with the Tao in the morning can die in peace in the evening."

Once we become adept at living the Tao, our fear of death will begin to fade. We will be comfortable with the reality that our life is no more significant than a footprint on the beach, and that eventually the sands of time will wipe away every trace of our existence. We will also come to understand that we never really die. We simply return to where we came from—the nameless Mother of the Ten Thousand Things—the eternal Tao.

Stilling the Mind

It is very difficult for most Westerners to be completely still for even a short period of time. We are constantly working, talking, or thinking. And when we aren't moving around or talking directly to another person, the television, radio, telephone, computer, or newspaper are talking to us. It is important that we learn to slow down, and as Alan Watts used to say, "lessen the chatter inside our skulls." When we are able to do this, we will begin to feel more connected to the rest of the universe.

Meditation, performed either sitting or walking, is a wonderful way to still the mind. As we lessen the chatter in our heads, we will begin to experience the world in a different way. Our senses will become more attuned to the subtle sights, sounds, and smells we often ignore in our hectic lives. It is important to point out that when we first begin these practices, many of the issues and feelings we have been pushing down can come up, and we may need some support to help process them.

The Taoist allows time each day to quietly observe the natural process, both inside him and around him. By stilling the mind, he exists completely in the here and now. By stilling the mind, he transcends the ego. By stilling the mind, he harmonizes with the great Tao.

Stillpoint

"Stillpoint" is an English translation of an old Chinese expression that means, "settled heart." We may wander, but we take our settled heart with us.

The Taoist is completely comfortable and at peace within her body. She knows there is nothing she has to do; there is nobody she has to become; there is no way she has to feel. She has reached her stillpoint. She has *become* the Tao.

References and Resources

References

I am greatly indebted to the following authors and translators, whose books, tapes, and lectures played an important role in helping me move forward in my recovery:

Recovery/Psychology

Melody Beattie; Claudia Black; Robert Bly; John Bradshaw; Patrick Carnes; Bob Earle; Terry Gorski; Robert Johnson; C.G. Jung; Ernie Larsen; John Lee; Pia Mellody; Anne Wilson Schaef.

Philosophy/Mythology

Joseph Campbell; Gia-fu Feng; Jane English; William Martin; Stephen Mitchell; Jacob Needleman; Brother David Stendl-Rast; Alan Watts.

Resources

The Electronic University; Hazelden Publications; Recovery World Bookstores; Sounds True Audios; Unity Church Bookstores; all other booksellers—large and small.